Jesus, This Is Your Prayer

The Lord's Prayer According to Kids

Edited by Jeff Kunkel

Augsburg Books
Bringing Families Together
for Children & Families

Our Father, who art in heaven,
hallowed be thy name, thy kingdom come,
thy will be done, on earth as it is in heaven.
Give us this day our daily bread;
and forgive us our trespasses,
as we forgive those who trespass against us;
and lead us not into temptation,
but deliver us from evil.
For thine is the kingdom, and the power, and the glory,
forever and ever. Amen"
Lutheran Book of Worship

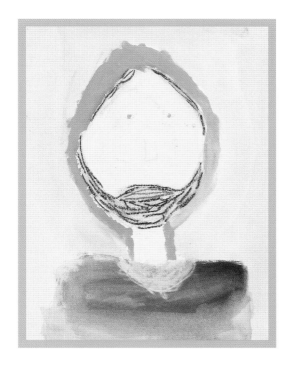

"This is Jesus. His face shines with a blue light from heaven."
—Ian Rowan, age 9

A Light Has Gone Out
Penny Penrose, 1949-2003

watercolor, by Penny Penrose

JESUS, THIS IS YOUR PRAYER
The Lord's Prayer According to Kids

Scripture passages are from the New Revised Standard Version of the Bible, copyright © 1946, 1952, 1971, 1989 by the Division of Christian Education of the National Council of the Churches of Christ in the USA. Used by permission.

Cover and book design by Michelle L. N. Cook

ISBN 0-8066-4403-6

The paper used in this publication meets the minimum requirements of American National Standard for Information Sciences—Permanence of Paper for Printed Library Materials, ANSI Z329.48-1984. ♾ ™

Printed in China

08   07   06   05   04   1   2   3   4   5   6   7   8   9   10

Contents

Introduction

Christians are a praying people, and one of the most beloved, familiar prayers in the Christian tradition is the Lord's Prayer or Our Father. It is an ancient prayer—first prayed by Christians more than two thousand years ago. The writers of the New Testament of the Bible knew the prayer, and they tell us that Jesus himself taught this prayer to his first disciples. Did Jesus teach them this prayer in English? No! English wasn't invented yet. Jesus taught this prayer in the language used by his family and disciples, a language called Aramaic. But many people did not know Aramaic, so the prayer was translated into other languages spoken at the time, like Greek and Latin. Five hundred years ago, the Lord's Prayer was first translated into English. Today, the Lord's Prayer has been translated into nearly every language on earth.

While there are many books that introduce and explore the Lord's Prayer, this is the first book that explores the Lord's Prayer according to kids, using the words and pictures of dozens of children. These children attended one of my StoryArt workships. They ranged in age from four to fifteen and came from several states and many racial, ethnic, and religious backgrounds. Some of these children already knew the Lord's Prayer by heart—others had never heard it until I read it to them. Very few had ever been asked to illustrate or translate the Lord's Prayer into their own words.

Here's what I did in my workshops: I read the Lord's Prayer out loud, several times, in different translations. Because the prayer was first taught by a grown-up Jesus to

"This is my picture of Jeff Kunkel."
—Armando Saavedra, age 8

his grown-up disciples, the prayer uses some grown-up words not familiar to most children, such as "hallowed," "trespasses," and "temptation." I took these adult words, one by one, and together, the children and I talked about what these words mean.

Many children wanted to know what made the Lord's Prayer different from other prayers. I answered them this way: First, the Lord's Prayer is the only prayer that we know about that Jesus taught to his first disciples, word for word. Second, the Lord's Prayer addresses God in an up-close, personal way, as "Father" or "Parent." Third, the Lord's Prayer never uses the words "I" or "me" or "mine," but rather uses the words "we" and "us" and "our."

I asked each child to print or write the Lord's Prayer in his or her own words. Then, with their own translations of the prayer before them, I asked them to explore the Lord's Prayer phrase by phrase, through conversation, drawing, and painting. What these children imagined, discovered, and expressed is now before you in this book. Let their words and pictures inspire you to learn more about the prayer Jesus taught us.

Jeff Kunkel

Jeff Kunkel

What Is Prayer?

Prayer is the way we talk to God, the way we thank God, and the way we show our love to God."
—Lexi Loessburg-Zahl, age 8

"When I want to make God my friend, I talk to him like he's right next to me. That's what prayer is."
—Alysandre Saavedra, age 11

"Prayer clears the mind and gets us ready to receive God's blessings."
—Malia Bishop, age 10

"Prayer is when you talk to God. You can say a prayer in your head or out loud. You can say a prayer with your eyes closed or open. You can say a prayer when you're all alone or in the middle of a crowd. You can say a prayer in church, at home, or anywhere at all."
—Jacob Ingle, age 10

"Kindness and love coming down on a person praying."
—Katy Ten-Hove, age 8

"This is one way to pray, by putting
your hands together and closing your eyes."
—Sergio Canchola, age 9

What Is the Lord's Prayer?

*The Lord's Prayer is the prayer which Jesus taught his first followers,
as we find out in this Bible story: Matthew 6:5-15*

written by Alysandre Saavedra, age 11

Once, Jesus said to his followers, "When you pray, do not pray like the show-offs. They pray in public so that lots of people will see them and think that they love God. But when you pray, go to your room and pray in secret, with the door closed. Your Father in heaven, who lives in secret and looks in secret, will reward you. And don't heap up long, empty phrases like so many others do. Make your phrases simple and from the heart, full of meaning and love. And when you pray, pray like this:

Our Maker,
Who lives in Heaven,
Sacred by your Name.
May your will happen on earth
just as it does in Heaven.
Give us each day
our daily meals
and forgive us our sin
as we forgive those who have sinned against us.
Please don't lead us into temptation,
and steer us away from evil
For yours is the Kingdom, the Power, and the Glory forever.
Amen"

"This is Jesus teaching his
disciples to pray."
—Lizzy Ten-Hove, age 10

"This is a picture of four
women praying in church"
—Emma Covington, age 8

"I'm praying in my room, with my
arm raised to God."
—Leah Floccare, age 6

"A person praying
and God listening."
—Takumi Murayama, age 10

Our Father, Who Lives in Heaven

In the Lord's Prayer, God is named in an up-close, personal way, as the one who takes care of us.

Our Daddy in Heaven . . ."
—Gracie Francisco, age 9

"Father and Mother of us all . . ."
—Hikari Murayama, age 8

"Our Lover . . ."
—Zahra Gifford, age 10

"Our Loving Parent Who Lives in Heaven . . ."
—Josh Loessburg-Zahl, age 10

"We studied Greek sculptures of gods in schools, so I painted God the Father in this way."
—Doyle Niu, age 12

—Caitlin Gifford, age 14

"The green is a cloud under heaven—the red is a mountain in heaven, and God is in pink, climbing the mountain. Even in heaven, we can climb mountains with God our Father."
—Chris Major, age 13

"This is Mrs. God and an angel in heaven. Mr. God is away, taking care of the children."
—Kayla Ingle, age 8

Holy Be Your Name!

Y ou are so awesome!"
—Holly Myer, age 15

"Shine down your name in light!"
—Mackenzie Covington, age 10

"Praise and Worship will be your name!"
—Kilan Bishop, age 12

"God's holy light shining in the darkness."
—Colin Davis, age 11

"Two people honoring God, the Holy One."
—Erica Ramos-Thompson, age 10

Your Kingdom Come, Your Will Be Done, on Earth As in Heaven

M ake earth like heaven."
—Lexi Loessberg-Zahl, age 8

"Heaven approach!"
—Kilan Bishop, age 12

"On earth as it is up high . . ."
—Jacob Ingle, age 10

"Heaven is peaceful, like the clouds, and blue, like the sky."
—Valerie Major, age 11

"God's kingdom, above, is at peace. The earth, below, is at war.
In the Lord's Prayer, we ask God to make earth more like heaven."
—Ian Cowan, age 10

"God (in red) coming down out of heaven
to make earth more like heaven."
—Lexi Loessburg-Zahl, age 8

"This is a person going up from earth to live in heaven."
—Melissa Sidener, age 7

Give Us This Day Our Daily Bread

G ive us what we need."
—Malia Bishop, age 10

"Thank you for this day—it's been great having you in my heart. . . ."
—Ruth Niu, age 9

"Keep our health up."
—Malia Bishop, age 10

"God keeps us strong!"
—Robbie Ferguson, age 8

"God gives us the food we need."
—Holly Myer, age 15

"This is a white loaf
of bread."
—Lizzy Ten-Hove, age 10

"Give us our daily bread."
—Lucy Barthel, age 7

"God is the baker. He is
baking our daily bread."
—Gus Hardy, age 9

"Water, bread, and a table
with grapes."
—Kayla Ingle, age 8

"A hungry girl (me) as God says, 'Have some bread.'"
—Katy Ten-Hove, age 8

"This is *my* plate, with plums, apple, bananas, green beans."
—Armando Saavedra, age 8

"My dinner plate, with chocolate milk, banana, apple, cheese roll, turkey leg, and peas."
—John Lovejoy, age 9

"God teaches us to share bread too!"
—Alysandre Saavedra, age 11

Forgive Us Our Trespasses, As We Forgive Those Who Trespass against Us

Forgive us our wrongs, as we forgive those who wrong us . . ."
—Renee Jaquith, age 10

"Forgive us our sins, as we forgive the ones who sin against us . . ."
—Rachel Assink, age 11

"Forgive us the bad things we do, as we forgive the bad things people do to us . . ."
—Lexi Loessburg-Zahl, age 8

"Forgiveness comes from the heart."
—Katie James, age 11

"This picture shows some of the ways people trespass. Upper left:
a person is snowmobiling on private property. Upper right: a person
is yelling at another person. Lower left: a car passing across a yellow,
do-not-pass line. Lower right: a person beating up someone. When
we forgive someone, we say, 'I won't hold your trespass against you.'"
—Myles Jellison, age 10

Lead Us Not into Temptation

L ead us away from what we want but aren't supposed to have."
—Elliott Tan, age 10

"Keep us away from the bad stuff."
—Holly Myer, age 15

"Don't give us problems that are too hard. . . ."
—Matthew Strasser, age 10

"Lead us not into temptation . . ."
—Christopher Aiken-Forderer, age 9

"Jesus was tempted to do bad things, just like we are.
This is Jesus being tempted by the devil, who says, 'Jesus, I'll give you
all kinds of good stuff if you obey me rather than God.'
Jesus said, 'No thanks. Get away from me!'"

"This is inside a person's mind. God helps the mind say 'No!' to bad things and 'Yes!' to good things."
—Alysandre Saavedra, age 11

"If we do too many bad things, we might get to heaven and see a big flashing sign which says, 'Access denied!'"
—Johnathan Khaleel, age 8

Deliver Us from Evil

K eep us away from Satan . . ."
—Hikari Murayama, age 8

"Keep us safe from the hot one."
—Angelica Sidener, age 9

"Deliver us from the fallen angel . . ."
—Erica Ramos-Thompson, age 10

"Guide us to the heavens . . ."
—Colin Davis, age 10

"Smiling devil."
—Noah Aust, age 10

"This is the devil's face. He has black eyes and mouth, with red blood coming out of his mouth."
—Shadrach Mateialona, age 9

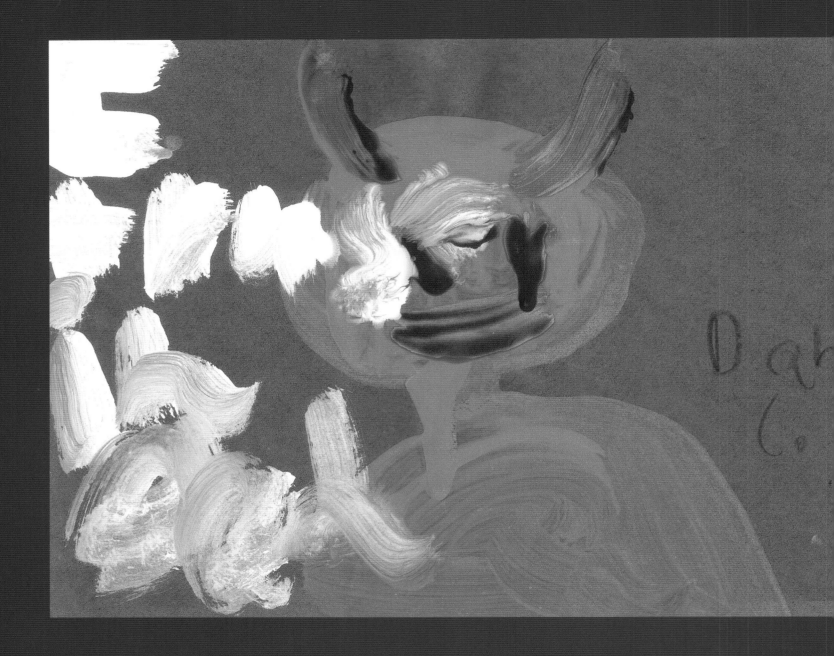

"The devil, with horns. He can become invisible too!"
—Dan Cowan, age 7

"This is the devil with huge wings and a pitchfork."
—Aisha Ivery, age 13

Yours Is the Kingdom, the Power, and the Glory Forever. Amen

Y ou are our home and our happiness, even after the end of the world."
—Melissa Buckley, age 10

"You are my light, my quick, my strength."
—Mackenzie Covington, age 10

"Amen! Alleluia! Hosanna!"
—Lizzy Ten-Hove, age 10

"So be it!"
—Erica Ramos-Thompson, age 10

"Forever."
—Jenna Mowat, age 8

"The gates of heaven. Whenever God opens
these gates, good things come out."
—Emily Burges-Weidemann, age 8

"This is God, who lives in heaven and earth.
God is about to stomp on the devil!"
—Noah Aust, age 10

"That's heaven on the right, with God sitting in a chair.
Every day, God sends angels from heaven to help out on earth."
—Ian Cowan, age 10

The Lord's Prayer in the Words of Kids

Our only God,
Father and Mother of us all,
please show yourself.
Do what's best, above as below,
Let us have our three meals.
Forgive us and help us forgive others.
Do not bring us to hard times
but keep us away from Satan.
For God is strong and has the glory.
Amen
—Hikari Murayama, age 8

Our Father,
He's in Heaven,
He's the Best.
His wishes come true on earth
Like they already have in heaven.
He will feed us
and will forgive us like we forgive others.
And everything will be great!
If Satan comes
God will tie him to a stick,
and everybody will throw rotten eggs at him.
And he will whine, as usual,
and he will have a horrible time.
But not us!
'Cuz God is so good!
Amen
—Noah Aust, age 10

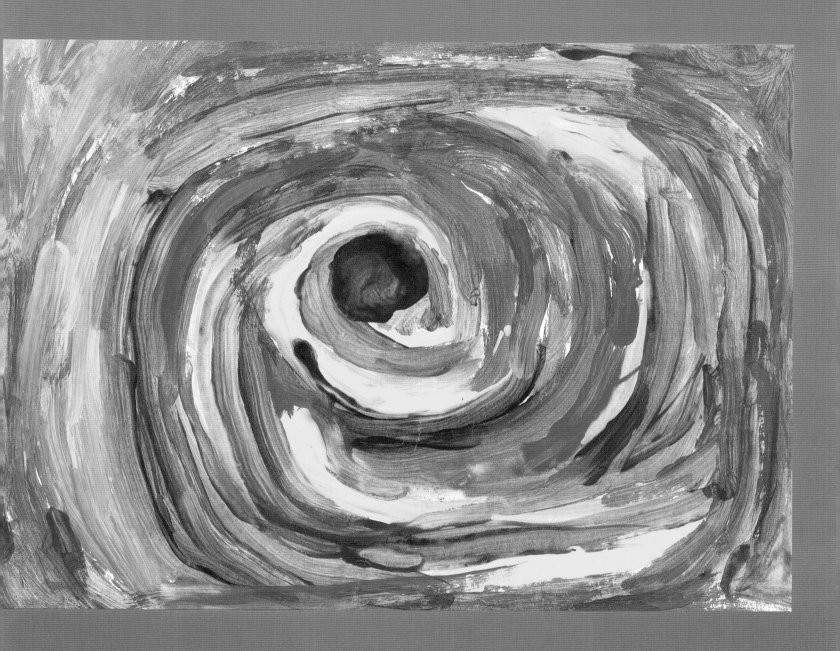

"God is the black at the center of the swirling color."
—Emilia McCann, age 7

Our Creator,
Who looks over and protects us,
praise and worship be your name.
Heaven approach! Your wishes be attended to
Keep food on the table.
Forgive us our flaws as we forgive those who have flaws among us.
Give us our own minds.
Do not let us follow others, but lead.
For yours is an eternal joy.
Hallelujah!
—Kilan Bishop, age 12

Our Dad,
Who is in heaven.
Keep our day holy.
Your Kingdom come.
Your will be done
on earth as it is in heaven.
Give us our daily bread
and forgive us like we forgive others.
Lead us not into evil,
but deliver us from Satan.
For you are a kingdom, a power,
and a goodness—forever!
—Shadrach Mateialona, age 9

"The Lord's Prayer was taught to us by Jesus."
—Calvin Barthel, age 10

The Lord's Prayer
in the Words of Adults

Our Father who Art in heaven,
Hallowed be thy name.
Thy kingdom come,
Thy will be done,
On earth as it is in heaven.
Give us this day our daily bread
And forgive us our debts,
As we also have forgiven our debtors;
And lead us not into temptation,
But deliver us from evil.
—Revised Standard Bible, 1954

Our Father in heaven:
May your holy name be honored;
may your kingdom come;
may your will be done on earth
as it is in heaven.
Give us today the food we need.
Forgive us the wrongs we have done,
as we forgive the wrongs
that others have done to us.
Do not bring us to hard testing,
but keep us safe from the Evil One.
—Good News Bible, 1976

"This is God our Father. He's so big that his head is in heaven and his legs are on earth. That's a white cloud around his knees.
—Daniel Sanghyun Park, age 10

Our Father in heaven
Reveal who you are.
Do what's best—as above, so below.
Keep us alive with three square meals.
Keep us forgiven with you and forgiving others,
Keep us safe from ourselves and the Devil.
You're in charge!
You can do anything you want!
You're ablaze in beauty!
Yes. Yes. Yes.
—Eugene Peterson's Bible, The Message, 2002

Our Father which art in heaven,
Hallowed be thy name.
Thy kingdom come.
Thy will be done in earth, as it is in heaven.
Give us this day our daily bread.
And forgive us our debts, as we forgive our debtors.
And lead us not into temptation, but deliver us from evil:
For thine is the kingdom, and the power, and the glory, for ever.
Amen
—King James Version, 1611

"This is the bread God gives us each day. On a table.
It's just regular bread, but in a way, it comes from heaven."
—Chrissy Talbot, age 10

Writers and Artists

Katie Reuter, age 12, Walnut Creek, CA, cover
Ian Rowan, age 9, Oakland, CA, 3
Armando Saavedra, age 8, San Jose, CA, 6, 25
Lexi Loessburg-Zahl, age 8, Elk Grove, CA, 8, 18, 20
Alysandre Saavedra, age 11, San Jose, CA, 8, 10, 25, 30
Malia Bishop, age 10, Sacramento, CA, 8, 22
Jacob Ingle, age 10, Citrus Heights, CA, 8, 18
Katy Ten-Hove, age 8, Albany, CA, 8, 25
Sergio Canchola, age 9, Sacramento, CA, 9
Lizzy Ten-Hove, age 10, Albany, CA, 11, 24, 36
Leah Floccare, age 6, Wauconda, IL, 11
Takumi Murayama, age 10, Kensington, CA, 11
Emma Covington, age 8, Pleasant Hill, CA, 11
Gracie Francisco, age 9, San Anselmo, CA, 12
Hikari Murayama, age 8, Kensington, CA, 12
Zahra Gifford, age 10, Sacramento, CA, 12
Josh Loessburg-Zahl, age 10, Elk Grove, CA, 12
Doyle Niu, age 12, Escalon, CA, 12
Caitlin Gifford, age 14, Sacramento, CA, 13
Chris Major, age 13, Santa Rosa, CA, 14
Kayla Ingle, age 8, Sacramento, CA, 15, 24
Holly Myer, age 15, Rancho Cordova, CA, 16, 23, 28
Mackenzie Covington, age 10, Pleasant Hill, CA, 16, 36
Kilan Bishop, age 12, Sacramento, CA, 16, 18, 42
Colin Davis, age 11, San Leandro, CA, 16, 32
Erica Ramos-Thompson, age 10, Oakland, CA, 17, 32, 36
Valerie Major, age 11, Santa Rosa, CA, 18
Ian Cowan, age 10, Oakland, CA, 19, 39
Melissa Sidener, age 7, Walton, CA, 21
Ruth Niu, age 9, Escalon, CA, 22
Robbie Ferguson, age 8, Crystal Lake, IL, 22
Lucy Barthel, age 7, Albany, CA, 24
Gus Hardy, age 9, Berkeley, CA, 24
John Lovejoy, age 9, Crystal Lake, IL, 25
Renee Jaquith, age 10, Richmond, CA, 26
Rachel Assink, age 11, Walnut Creek, CA, 26
Katie James, age 11, Hayward, CA, 26

Myles Jellison, age 10, Sacramento, CA, 27
Elliott Tan, age 10, Oakland, CA, 28
Matthew Strasser, age 10, Alameda, CA, 28
Christopher Aiken-Forderer, age 9, Los Altos, CA, 28
Chrissy Talbot, age 10, Oakland, CA, 29, 47
Johnathan Khaleel, age 8, Sacramento, CA, 31
Hikari Murayama, age 8, Kensington, CA, 32, 40
Angelica Sidener, age 9, Walton, CA, 32
Noah Aust, age 10, Oakland, CA, 32, 38, 40
Shadrach Mateialona, age 9, Hayward, CA, 33, 42
Dan Cowan, age 7, Oakland, CA, 34
Aisha Ivery, age 13, El Cerrito, CA, 35
Melissa Buckley, age 10, Oakland, CA, 36
Jenna Mowat, age 8, Piedmont, CA, 36
Emily Burges-Weidemann, age 8, Albany, CA, 37
Emilia McCann, age 7, Sacramento, CA, 41
Calvin Barthel, age 10, San Leandro, CA, 43
Daniel Sanghyun Park, age 10, Brentwood, CA, 45

Jeff Kunkel and some StoryArt kids.